Endorse

"I found Audrey's book very refreshing because she is not one of the 'downtrodden.' She opened up this very beautiful passage of Scripture which wonderfully expressed the liberty and dignity of women from God's perspective."

—Phil Edwards, Senior Pastor
Hope Community Church
Perivale, London

"Audrey Linton is a motivator and encourager, a woman of substance who lives by her principles. She is a woman who encourages you to aspire to be the best you can be. She writes with a prophetic edge. I would recommend Audrey's new book to you."

—Maureen Gordon
Author
Co-founder of Hope Tree

"Audrey Linton is a devoted and passionate writer who skillfully blends Christianity with business, resulting in highly inspirational messages that are truly uplifting. Audrey is a master in her own right destined for literary greatness."

—David F Roberts
Chief Executive Officer
CaribDirect Multi-Media Limited

P31 WOMEN

Ancient Secrets for Today's Women Leaders

P31 WOMEN

Ancient Secrets for Today's Women Leaders

AUDREY LINTON

TATE PUBLISHING
AND ENTERPRISES, LLC

Published by Tate Publishing & Enterprises, LLC
127 E. Trade Center Terrace | Mustang, Oklahoma 73064 USA
1.888.361.9473 | www.tatepublishing.com

Tate Publishing is committed to excellence in the publishing industry. The company reflects the philosophy established by the founders, based on Psalm 68:11,
"The Lord gave the word and great was the company of those who published it."

Book design copyright © 2016 by Tate Publishing, LLC. All rights reserved.
Cover design by Joana Quilantang
Interior design by Shieldon Alcasid

Published in the United States of America

ISBN: 978-1-68237-582-2
Religion / Devotional
15.11.23

This book is dedicated to Edna Robb

Granma, you lived in obscurity
In hills far away surrounded by the Caribbean Sea.
You became the mother of many,
Although only one sucked upon your breast
And drew energy and sustenance from what you possessed.

Granma, I remember you upon your death bed
Helpless, but not hopeless
Unknown, but well-known
Unable to live, but forever giving
Your life represented P31 Women.

Who can find a virtuous wife?
You'll find her in the hills giving life.
Enterprising, energising,
Called blessed by her inheritance,
Beautified by grace, touching the human race.

Proverbs 31

The sayings of King Lemuel—an inspired utterance his mother taught him.

2 Listen, my son! Listen, son of my womb!
    Listen, my son, the answer to my prayers!
3 Do not spend your strength on women,
    your vigour on those who ruin kings.
4 It is not for kings, Lemuel—
    it is not for kings to drink wine,
    not for rulers to crave beer,
5 lest they drink and forget what has been decreed,
    and deprive all the oppressed of their rights.
6 Let beer be for those who are perishing,
    wine for those who are in anguish!
7 Let them drink and forget their poverty
    and remember their misery no more.
8 Speak up for those who cannot speak for themselves,
    for the rights of all who are destitute.
9 Speak up and judge fairly;
    defend the rights of the poor and needy.

¹⁰ A wife of noble character who can find?
  She is worth far more than rubies.
¹¹ Her husband has full confidence in her
  and lacks nothing of value.
¹² She brings him good, not harm,
  all the days of her life.
¹³ She selects wool and flax
  and works with eager hands.
¹⁴ She is like the merchant ships,
  bringing her food from afar.
¹⁵ She gets up while it is still night;
  she provides food for her family
  and portions for her female servants.
¹⁶ She considers a field and buys it;
  out of her earnings she plants a vineyard.
¹⁷ She sets about her work vigorously;
  her arms are strong for her tasks.
¹⁸ She sees that her trading is profitable,
  and her lamp does not go out at night.
¹⁹ In her hand she holds the distaff
  and grasps the spindle with her fingers.
²⁰ She opens her arms to the poor
  and extends her hands to the needy.
²¹ When it snows, she has no fear for her household;
  for all of them are clothed in scarlet.
²² She makes coverings for her bed;
  she is clothed in fine linen and purple.

^{23} Her husband is respected at the city gate,
     where he takes his seat among the elders of the land.
^{24} She makes linen garments and sells them,
     and supplies the merchants with sashes.
^{25} She is clothed with strength and dignity;
     she can laugh at the days to come.
^{26} She speaks with wisdom,
     and faithful instruction is on her tongue.
^{27} She watches over the affairs of her household
     and does not eat the bread of idleness.
^{28} Her children arise and call her blessed;
     her husband also, and he praises her:
^{29} "Many women do noble things,
     but you surpass them all."
^{30} Charm is deceptive, and beauty is fleeting;
     but a woman who fears the LORD is to be praised.
^{31} Honour her for all that her hands have done,
     and let her works bring her praise at the city gate.

(*New International Version*)

Contents

Foreword

Many women have played a very significant and dominant role throughout biblical times.

This book is dedicated to outstanding biblical women, some of whom are unsung heroes, others stand tall within the annals of time for their wisdom, ingenuity, feminine influence and humility.

It draws on their virtues and wisdom and highlights the relevance of these virtues within today's society. Its themes recount that of the Proverbs 31 woman, let's call her "the P31 woman."

The P31 woman is either scorned or loved by women! To some, she epitomises the perfect woman—she is a loving wife, a caring mother, a homemaker; she's business focused, charitable, and well respected. Some women may believe they cannot relate to the P31 woman as she appears to be someone far beyond their scope and capacity to emulate. However, if we can lay aside, for a moment, this "image of perfection" and really get *"under the skin"* of this woman, then we'll see some characteristics and behaviours that we can all adopt and cultivate.

This book focuses on other biblical women who have shared some of these characteristics but who may have gone unnoticed or been attributed with little value within mainstream literary reviews of the day. I would like to share the stories of these women, which are based on facts, but interpreted so that today's women can gain greater insights into biblical women and celebrate the art of being a woman—being feminine, being strong yet vulnerable, being positive, compassionate, graceful, humble, wise, innovative, being directional, decision makers, influencers, great mothers, excellent wives, nurturers and leaders—this list is by no means exhaustive!

One phrase that holds these women in common esteem is that they were *life givers*. The term "life giver" can be interpreted in many ways, but as you read about the intricacies of these characters you will see that many of them gave spiritual as well as physical birth to future leaders, leaving lasting legacies as well as valuable life lessons which ultimately left an indelible impression on world history.

Who Should Read This Book?

The very fact that you are reading this book indicates that it is for you! You may be a woman in the workplace, a stay-at-home mum, a wife, or maybe a young woman just about to embark on life's adventure. You may be a biblical novice or biblically literate. Whatever your position, I hope you will gain some valuable insights from these women. You may even be a man who wants to understand the expansive gifts, talents, and skills of women and to celebrate the women in your life!

Whoever you are, this book is by no means intended to convey deep theology—I will leave that to the theologians! It is, however, the starting point for deeper exploration about who you are, the life you live, and the effect you have on others. Its aim is to help you draw on the God-given talents that are within you, enabling you to experience the richness within you and to challenge you to seek a deeper relationship with the greatest ever Life Giver, Jesus Christ.

As you read each chapter, enjoy the journey. Use the activities at the end of each chapter for a time of reflection and challenge and as a benchmark for a fulfilled life.

These writings are intended to encourage the reader to ask questions:

What does this mean for me?

What can I learn from these principles?

How can I apply these principles?

May the God of peace, love, and wisdom shine in you and through you so that you will connect in a greater way to your identity, call, and destiny.

Introduction

The P31 Woman: Who Was She?

As I was growing up, I always found Proverbs 31 very hard to relate to. Coming from a home in which the Bible played an important role in our library collection, it did not have the same excitement as the other Bible stories like Jonah in the belly of a whale, or Moses parting the Red Sea or even Eve, having a conversation with a snake!

The first ten verses of Proverbs 31 focus on a woman giving advice to her son—in fact, no ordinary son—he was a king. Some scholars believe that the king referred to here was King Solomon and his mother (Bathsheba), in her narrative, is giving him wise counsel about the appropriate behaviour of a leader. The mother's counsel advised him against the relentless pursuit of strange women, against the futility of reckless living, and against the evils of excessive alcohol consumption.

Instead, she encouraged him to seek the welfare of the terminally ill, to be a voice for the voiceless, and to prioritise administering justice.

Scholars are divided in their opinion as to whether the woman mentioned from verse 1–9 is the same woman from verse 10 onwards. Was it Solomon testifying of his mother or was this homage being paid to women in general? My personal belief is that she represented an allegory of the Bride of Christ, but that is a subject for another book!

Whoever she was, one thing we know: this woman is recorded and remembered throughout history.

From this point on, we will explore the principles and characteristics of the Proverbs 31 Woman by focusing on other biblical women who displayed similar characteristics of creativity, courage, decisiveness, and heroism in life-threatening situations.

Our focus will then reconnect to the woman mentioned in Proverbs 31 to uncover her entrepreneurial qualities which can help to inspire today's enterprising women. Finally, the focus will end with 'you,' the 'Designer's daughter,' you who are fearfully and wonderfully made, designed with purpose and for purpose.

1

The Mother of Life: Eve

Her husband has full confidence in her and lacks
nothing of value.

—Proverbs 31:11

Not much is known about Eve. She is remembered as the
wife of Adam who caused her husband to sin, thereby
causing the fall of the human race. It wasn't a very good
start for her, was it? In fact, it wasn't a very good start for
women as a whole, as the book of Genesis recounts that
because of her disobedience, the following distresses would
become the blight of all females who would ever be born:

- In pain, women would have children.

- Women would serve their husbands.

- Their sorrows in conception would be greatly
  multiplied!

- The wife would desire dominance over her husband, but the husband would dominate the wife (Genesis 3:16 paraphrased and author's interpretation).

Yes, women, not a very good start for us, was it?

Let us look more closely at Genesis 2 as it highlights the attributes that were bestowed upon Eve before she and her husband disobeyed God.

God is our ultimate Life Giver, but He has also endowed women with the power to give life.

"Eve" translated from the Hebrew script means "the mother of all living" (life spring and life giver). The name also means "to gleam," "to enlighten," "to admonish," "to shine," "to teach," "to warn," "brightness," and "brilliancy."[1]

It was Adam's responsibility to name his wife and he esteemed her by calling her Eve. She was the vessel which God used to literally bring forth life. It is the female that has the natural ability to birth life. Adam's responsibility was to name his wife—not to *call her names*. Words of life were spoken over her by Adam—she will gleam and enlighten, she will emanate brilliance and brightness as she maintains the office of life giver.

P31 women give life. They are called to shine with brightness and brilliance. Their role is not to compete with their male counterpart, but it is with his blessing they can fully be released to shine as he bestows honour upon her—and what honour!

---

[1]   Strong's Exhaustive Concordance of the Bible

According to Proverbs 31:11–12:

> Her husband has full confidence in her and lacks nothing of value.
>
> She brings him good, not harm, all the days of her life.

Why? Because he has recognised her purpose, that as she walks in her vocation as life giver, all who come into contact with her will be blessed.

There is a need for today's society to understand the true meaning of equality and to realise that releasing women to function in all the aspects to which they are called, will truly cause "Adam" to find his "help mete" or suitable life helper/partner.

The destiny that God has intended for the human race cannot be achieved by a single gender, but once we have realised our specific call, office, and function, God will indeed have full confidence in us to fulfil *His* original plan and purpose.

P31 Leadership Virtues

In what ways are you a *life giver* to others?

Is there anyone from whom you are withholding the gift of life, through unforgiveness, resentment, or competition?

What five things will you put in place to ensure you will be a fountain of life for others?

Find at least five men (father, brothers, sons, uncles, and friends) to whom you can bring honour. If you are married, think of five ways that you bring honour to your husband.

XXXXX

Seek out a coach, mentor, or confidant who will act as your life giver, who will replenish you when you are running on empty, someone who will be candid with you when they see you approaching a "no-go" area.

Father, forgive me if I have dishonoured the men you have placed in my life. I profess, I am a life giver.

2

The Midwives: Shiprah and Puah

A woman who fears the Lord is to be praised.

—Proverbs 31:30

Midwives play a vital role in the latter stages of a woman's confinement. If they undertake the delivery procedures incorrectly, they can cause permanent damage, even death, to both mother and infant. They have the ability to give life or take life.

There were two midwives who were fundamental in the emergence and survival of the Jewish people. They will be remembered throughout history because they dared to defy the Pharaoh of Egypt. Their names were Shiprah and Puah.

Shiphrah means "splendid," "tapestry," "royal pavilion," and Puah (ironically and notwithstanding the sound of the name) means "glitter," or "brilliance."[2]

---

[2] Strong's Exhaustive Concordance of the Bible

For those of you who are not familiar with the story of these two women, Exodus 2 recounts that the Israelites had settled in Egypt for many years due to the severe famine which had taken place over the known world. Joseph, the son of Israel, had orchestrated the arrival and settlement of his family into Egypt, but he had warned them that God would visit the Israelites again at which time they were to return to their land and take his (Joseph's) bones with them.

Little did they know that they would spend over 400 years in Egypt after the death of Joseph. Their new landlords made life extremely difficult for them because they recognised that God had made them prosperous. The children of Israel were fruitful and multiplied and grew exceedingly mighty in the land of Egypt.

There arose a new Pharaoh who was oblivious to the works of Joseph, and he perceived that the children of Israel would become a threat to him and his subjects. For that reason, he called on all Hebrew midwives and instructed them to kill all the newborn male Israelite babies, but to save the female babies.

The Hebrew midwives feared God and were aware of the destiny of the Hebrew people. They bravely opted to disobey the commands of Pharaoh and subsequently saved many lives. Pharaoh noticed that his instructions had not been followed and he questioned the midwives accordingly. I just love their response to this man of power and might. Their exquisite wisdom, respect, and integrity were uncompromised.

They reported to Pharaoh that the Hebrew women were so strong that by the time they arrived at the delivery chamber, the babies had already been born!

What could Pharaoh do? Absolutely nothing! These women were rewarded by the Lord for their shrewd decision to delay their attendance at the birth of the Hebrew women's children.

God honoured the midwives, blessed them, and gave them families of their own.

A woman who fears the Lord, she shall be praised!

P31 Leadership Virtues

Identify the "Pharaohs" in your life. How has "Pharaoh" compromised your position resulting in you having to make a decision about whether to listen to him or listen to your own conscience?

What will you lose if you do not obey?

How will you stand up to Pharaoh?

Prepare in writing what you will say and ask your confidant/coach or mentor to review it.

3

Getting Paid for What You Were Born to Do: The Mother of Moses

Listen, my son! Listen, son of my womb! Listen,
my son, the answer to my prayers!

—Proverbs 31:2

How many of you are in jobs or roles that you believe you were born to do? Hmm, probably not many hands going up at present!

Well, how's this for the wow factor: the mother of Moses, whose name was Jochebed, got paid for looking after her child.

I can hear you mothers saying, "Really, how did she do that? Was that a government initiative?"

Not at all, it was the result of a more supernatural rather than governmental intervention. Let me explain!

Pharaoh, King of Egypt, advised the Hebrew midwives to undertake the gruesome infanticide of every male Hebrew child as they were being born, but (as mentioned in the previous chapter) these midwives were noncompliant and delayed their attendance at the births of the Hebrew children.

Pharaoh's plan B was an edict to ensure all the male infants were thrown into the River Nile and drowned. One Hebrew mother was desperate to protect her child, so she came up with an innovative idea, which with hindsight, possibly verged on the brink of madness. However, this child was no ordinary child, this child was Moses, the assigned deliverer of the children of Israel.

She made a little ark, laid her baby in it, and placed the ark on the River Nile and just prayed that God would take care of the little one. Both Jochebed and her daughter Miriam watched as the ark drifted away. I am sure any mother would be distraught knowing that their child was left to the elements for survival—not these two women! Miriam had a different perspective.

Within minutes, lo and behold, Pharaoh's daughter went down to the river to take a bath—yes in the River Nile—the mind boggles! Traditionally, it was believed that the River Nile was possessed with supernatural power and therefore bathing in it would empower the Royals! Anyway, on with the story!

Pharaoh's daughter (let's call her "Miss Tut" for ease of reference) noticed the little ark drifting down the River Nile and she asked her maid to go and see what it contained. Now what turned up before her was a basket with a crying baby, yes baby Moses! Well, Miss Tut's maternal instinct rapidly came into play and she just fell in love with the little cutie.

Miriam, who was observing this from afar, immediately saw an opportunity and she quickly drew near to the Egyptian entourage and made a gallant suggestion.

She explained, "As this baby is a Hebrew baby, why don't I go and ask one of the Hebrew women to look after him for you?"

"Excellent idea!" Miss Tut exclaimed, "I will pay her well."

Within no time, Miriam went to call her mother to look after little Moses. Now as far as I am aware, Pharaoh's daughter did not know the carer was Moses' real mother, so she agreed to pay her for looking after Moses.

Now how was that for divine favour and intervention? Moses' mother was getting paid for looking after her own son!

So what is the moral of the story? In God's perfect timing and His perfect way, He will enable you to fulfill what you were born to do and you may even get paid for it. Your gift will make room for you.

The mother of Moses fulfilled her call in raising her son, instilling into him the key skills, beliefs, and characteristics which would prepare him for his great future mission. She also honoured Pharaoh's daughter by taking Moses back to the Palace once he became a certain age, but she had the opportunity of keeping her son alive and nursing him in his formative years.

Miriam changed the course and destiny of a nation through her sharp eye and quick thinking. Her influence was so far reaching that she planted the idea in Pharaoh's daughter's mind that the young child should be looked after by a Hebrew woman. Miriam saw the bigger picture as the ark sailed down the River Nile. She wasn't overcome by the hopelessness of the situation, but she took full advantage of her sphere of influence and enabled her mother to look after her son and get an income for doing so.

Unlike her father, Pharaoh's daughter showed deep compassion, and, no doubt, she knew she was defying her father's wishes. We could perhaps class her as one of the first human rights activists who wanted to fight for the protection of children. Whatever her role or title, she too had an amazing influence in this historical event.

If there is something that you believe you were born to do, then seek to pursue it; take that step of faith and the bridge will appear. If you are still trying to find your purpose, then consider what you already have; the seed of your purpose is usually already within you.

P31 Leadership Virtues

If you had the opportunity to fulfill all of your deepest dreams, what would they be?

Name the internal blockers (your self-limiting beliefs) that stand in your way?

Name the external blockers (forces outside your control) that stand in your way?

What three solutions would move you toward overcoming each blocker?

Discuss this with your coach.

4

He Loves Me, He Loves Me Not!
Leah and Rachel

She can laugh at the days to come.

—Proverbs 31:25

Here's the picture: one man, two women, and a devious father-in-law! Genesis 29 tells us that Jacob, the son of Isaac and Rebekah, worked for his uncle, Laban, for seven years so that he could marry Rachel, Laban's youngest daughter. On his wedding night, when he was ready to ravish his new bride, Laban told his older daughter, Leah, that she should go and sleep with Jacob instead. Jacob was probably in no state to know who was with him in his bed as he was probably heavily intoxicated after his wedding celebrations! Can you imagine the horror when Jacob woke up from his drunken stupor to find out that the woman he had worked seven years hard labour for was not the one that was lying next to him in his bed!

So let's pause for a while and explore this threesome and the role that these two sisters played in the bigger scheme of things.

Jacob loved Rachel more than Leah and on the scale of good looks, Rachel scored very high as she is described as being very beautiful. Leah on the other hand was described as tender eyed. It is not clear whether her eyes were delicate and soft or whether she had a slight squint and was perhaps a little cockeyed! Whatever the meaning, she was not Jacob's first choice, but Laban insisted that the elder sister should marry before the younger, and as a result, Jacob negotiated with Laban that he would work another seven years for Rachel, if Laban would allow him to marry her. So in total, Jacob worked fourteen years for these two women and ended up with two wives.

Are you with me so far? Good!

Why I love this story so much is the fact that although Leah was not loved by Jacob—and she knew it—yet she bore Jacob six of his twelve sons. Genesis 29:31–35 sums things up nicely with the proclamations at the birth of her first four sons:

> When GOD realized that Leah was unloved, he opened her womb. But Rachel was barren. Leah became pregnant and had a son. She named him Reuben (Look-It's-a-Boy!). "This is a sign," she said, "that GOD has seen my misery; and a sign that now my husband will love me."

She became pregnant again and had another son. "GOD heard," she said, "that I was unloved and so he gave me this son also." She named this one Simeon (GOD-Heard). She became pregnant yet again— another son. She said, "Now maybe my husband will connect with me—I've given him three sons!" That's why she named him Levi (Connect). She became pregnant a final time and had a fourth son. She said, "This time I'll praise GOD." So she named him Judah (Praise-GOD). Then she stopped having children.

(*The Message*)

Why would God honour Leah in this way?

The way I see it, God always fights for the underdog! Perhaps Leah grew up knowing she wasn't beautiful— she may never have had a second glance from a man, and (obviously) she wasn't Jacob's first choice. Her first three sons were given names which highlighted her pain of being unloved:

'Wow, I have borne my husband a boy! Surely he will love me.'

'God has heard my cry, my husband must love me now?'

'I have given him three sons—this time, my husband will connect with me.'

After an exhausting pursuit for the love of her husband, finally at the birth of her fourth son, her narrative changed. She may have thought:

"It doesn't matter if I am not loved by someone whom I love. I've tried to win my husband's love, but it just hasn't worked. All I know is that I am loved by God, and His love is sufficient for me, so I will just praise Him no matter what situation I find myself in. My son Judah will also be a reflection of how much God loves me and I will praise Him no matter what turmoil seems to be going on in my life."

Readers, praise is one of the keys to success. An attitude of gratitude releases endorphins throughout the body, which will enable you to change your whole outlook on life. I believe it was Leah's "aha" moment, which enabled her to call her son Praise. It was through the lineage of Praise (Judah) that the Messiah came.

A daily dose of praise and gratitude is key for today's leaders. Be grateful for the people you are connected to and who are part of your circle of friends and acquaintances. Learn to thank your workforce, your team, your congregation more. Be generous with your praise, especially to God.

The story of Rachel and Leah highlighted sibling rivalry and jealousy, it also highlighted the pain of both women, as initially Rachel could not have children. God eventually honoured her and she had two sons: Joseph, who went on to do great things as Prime Minister of Egypt, and Benjamin.

It is also interesting to note that at his death, Jacob was buried with Leah, not Rachel—the man who wanted to spend a lifetime with Rachel, ended up spending eternity with Leah!

P31 Leadership Virtues

Have you ever felt unloved? What were your coping strategies?

Is there anyone that you have been jealous of? What do you need to do to release yourself from that jealousy?

What strategies will you adopt to develop a grateful and thankful attitude?

Find at least five people that you can praise today.

5

Stand Up for Your Rights!
The Daughters of Zelophehad

> Speak up for those who cannot speak for
> themselves, for the rights of all who are destitute.
>
> —Proverbs 31:8

Do you want to bring about change to a given situation but often feel powerless to do so? Maybe you see injustice, unfairness, and inequality in your workplace, business, neighbourhood, or even your place of worship!

I am fascinated by the story of five women who were probably the first agents of change and were instrumental in levelling the playing field between men and women. These women were called the Daughters of Zelophehad.

"The daughters of who?" I hear you say. "The Daughters of Zelophehad" (Numbers 27).

Let me explain! Now in my opinion, I think it's fair to say society seemed pretty much male-dominated in ancient times under the leadership of Moses, and I give all due respect to our brothers! But traditionally during those times, any inheritance of land from the father was usually passed down to the firstborn male, alternatively if the firstborn was female, the inheritance would still be awarded to the male regardless of the level of the pecking order. In addition to this, if there were no male children in the family and only female, then any inheritance would be passed over to auction and be divided amongst other tribes, but not among the womenfolk!

Now, ladies, I know you are saying, "That's not fair!" Well, that's exactly what these five women thought. After the death of their father, the daughters convened a family meeting to discuss how they would tackle this injustice and they wanted to bring this matter to the CEO's attention, better known as Moses.

I don't know about you, but I get a little agitated when I experience injustice, and sometimes, my approach is not always conducive to solving the issue but possibly serves more to exacerbate it! However, these five women—Malah, Noa, Milcah, Tirzah, and Hoglah—were a little more gracious than I and their approach was meticulously planned, thought through, respectful, and compliant with the culture of the day inasmuch as they submitted to their elders.

Before they approached Moses and the other elders, they no doubt researched the topic: "How to Deal with Conflict When the Status Quo Is Challenged?" Then, in the spirit of meekness, yet with the boldness of lions, and as any good lawyer would, they stated their case, highlighted the facts, and backed up their argument. I can just imagine the court scene now, the following serves to paraphrase their opening statement:

> "Our father died without having borne sons, yet why should the name of our father become obsolete merely because he had no sons and we are unmarried women? Surely we too deserve an assignment of property along with the rest of our relatives?"
>
> "But you are women, you're not entitled to an inheritance," Moses reminded them.
>
> "But why not?" questioned the daughters.
>
> "Well because the law doesn't state that," responded Moses.
>
> "Well surely we serve a God of justice, mercy and compassion, is it not possible for you to seek God on the matter? Please!" Milcah responded firmly.

I think Moses had learned at an early age—especially growing up with his mother, his sister, and in the presence of Pharaoh's daughter—not to argue with a woman! When they get something in their head, they are as tenacious as a dog with a bone, so before he made any hasty decisions, he thought best to seek supernatural advice from the Almighty.

Well, would you believe it, the God of justice agreed with the women and He instructed Moses to immediately take action and change any law that discriminates against women having an inheritance.

These transformational events were so significant that they paved the way for future generations, not only to gain access to their inheritance, but they also brought about amendments to current legislation allowing wider eligibility for relatives to share in their clan's inheritance.

Now what can we learn from this?

Firstly, resolving conflict not only necessitates the presentation of evidence and facts, but equally important is a right attitude and approach to gain a win-win situation.

Secondly, to bring about change requires a common and shared vision or aim. Notwithstanding, there may be a period of time when you have to stand alone.

Just imagine if our present-day heroes failed to stand up for what they instinctively knew was right.

If Martin Luther King Jr. had settled in his zone of comfort rather than march to Washington for equality and justice, he, and indeed we, would never know "he had a dream."

If Nelson Mandela grew bitter and twisted whilst in his tiny prison cell on Robben Island, he would never have admonished us in his inauguration speech: "Our deepest fear is not that we are inadequate...but that we are powerful beyond measure..."

If Rosa Parks had given way to the taunts of her fellow white bus passengers, she would never have written: "Knowing what must be done does away with fear."

If Jesus Christ had decided that the road to Calvary was far too painful, we would never have heard His prayer: "Father, forgive them, for they know not what they do."

The courage of the Daughters of Zelophehad caused, even forced, a paradigm shift, moved God and man, and they became world changers.

P31 Leadership Virtues

The challenge: what cause have you stood up for lately?

What struggles of injustice have you encountered personally and professionally? How did you address them?

Could you have dealt with this differently?

Identify three strategies which you could use to achieve a positive outcome should you encounter these injustices again?

6

The Leadership Secrets of the Queen Bee: Deborah

Speak up and judge fairly; defend the rights of the
poor and needy.

—Proverbs 31:9

Perhaps you are wondering what bees have to do with leadership? Come with me for a short while as I share with you my thoughts on the leadership secrets of the queen bee.

The Bible says, "The Children of Israel did evil in the sight of the Lord." In other words, they were up to no good again! Not such a far cry from the things that go on in our society today! As a consequence, they were oppressed by the Canaanite people. During this time, the children of Israel were without a king, president, or prime minister to provide leadership and strategic direction. This was the ideal time to turn to God as their only true king and to seek his wisdom, but this did not happen. This was a grave mistake as it is one thing to conquer territory, but it is another to build infrastructure, laws, rules, political systems, and governance to establish a society and ensure its longevity.

Never underestimate the power of wise leadership during times of transition.

In the conspicuous absence of careful administration, long-term planning and goal setting, chaos will be the by-product and people will be doing whatever *they feel* is right to do and who could blame them!

The book of Judges recounts that whilst Israel was without a monarchy it was governed by a selection of Judges whose roles were to bring governmental stability to the nation and to develop and fortify its military force. However, the underlying need was for the Judges to ensure the nation kept their focus and dependence on the Lord God Almighty who had freed them from slavery and settled them into the land that they had been promised.

One such Judge was Deborah, who governed Israel around 1107–1067 BC. To set things into context, this was a very difficult time in the children of Israel's history.

As well as being one of the ancient judiciary leaders in Israel's history, she was a wife and mother and also held the privileged position of being a Prophetess (one able to foretell the future). Suffice to say, a very high profile position.

Her 'place of work' was usually under a palm tree. She was also an astute business woman and a landowner and people would go to her for her to arbitrate and judge their cases. Deborah was appointed as Judge to Israel at a time when they were being oppressed by one of their greatest enemies, the Canaanites. They were a force to be reckoned with and their mighty army was led by Sisera, who had over 900 iron chariots. I suppose we could liken this to modern-day weapons of mass destruction!

At that time, Barak was the commander-in-chief of Israel's army, and one day, Deborah gave him a message from the Lord.

"Barak, I have a message for you from God," professed Deborah. "Gather your warriors from two of Israel's tribes, Naphtali and Zebulun, onto Mount Tabor and God will ensure that He leads your enemies, the Canaanites, into your hands."

Barak spluttered and anxiously said, "Not likely, I'm not going to fight that bulldog unless you go with me!" (*author's paraphrase*).

Was this the commander of Israel's army quaking in his boots? Did we hear correctly? Was he saying that unless Deborah, a wife and mother, fought the battle with him, he would not even consider challenging the might of the Canaanites? Yes, that's what he said!

Barak did not want to fight this battle without Deborah as he depended upon her connection with the Lord to help Israel win the battle. So what was it about Deborah that made her so special? Perhaps the secret may be in her name?

The Arabic meaning of Deborah is "bee"—"honeybee" to be precise. This might be a telltale sign of the reason why she was not only a chosen leader but had the reputation of a fearless one.

Well, let's examine the way of the bee:

Bees Produce Honey

Honey is a natural sweetener and is also high in nutrition. Containing most of the vitamins and minerals needed by humans, it provides energy and nurtures.

Could that be how Deborah spent her time under the palm tree, being an energy giver, nurturing, and sweetening conflict-torn lives? Remember the Canaanites had oppressed Israel for many years. The Israelites were probably worn down by this relentless oppression.

Bees Carry Pollen

Pollen is the powder inside flowers which, when transferred, fertilises other flowers. Can you imagine how this judge and prophetess would "fertilise" those that came to her every day for advice and guidance?

Bees Are Interdependent and Live in Colonies

The queen bee, worker bee, and drones are all dependent on each other for survival. They prefer hives that are clean, dry and protected from the weather. Deborah's mission was to empower and she collaborated with Israel's military leader in order to fulfill a mission. She respected delegated authority and recognised the difference between what she was assigned to do and what she was *not* assigned to.

The Queen Bee is Carefully Prepared to Reproduce

The queen bee is the mother of most bees in the hive. She cares for her offspring and her function is to reproduce. Deborah was a giver of life.

Bees Sting

The queen bee can sting any antagonist repeatedly without dying. As a prophetess, there were times that Deborah's word would probably carry a sharp sting, but her sting was not to destroy but to give life. Like a surgeon's scalpel, her judgments were fair and just and designed to foster wholeness and harmony.

Bees Do Not See Red

Red is often associated with danger. Deborah did not consider the mission assigned to Barak as dangerous. She was extremely confident in knowing that God would be true to his word and give the Canaanites into the hands of Israel.

P31 Leadership Virtues

What leadership lessons can we learn from the queen bee?

Leaders nurture.

Is there anyone in your sphere of influence that you need to nurture: feed, support, encourage, mentor, protect?

Who are they?

Where do they live?

What one step will you take to ensure this happens?

How will you become an energy giver to this person(s)?

Leaders are interdependent.
None of us can fulfill our call and life's work on our own. Who do you need to form partnerships and alliances with to ensure you fulfill your mission?

What will you need to do to manage your differences?

Leaders grow potential leaders.
Who are you mentoring and grooming to be more successful than you?

Leaders overcome the fear of failure.

Failure and learning from failure is one of the key ingredients of good leadership.

7

The Nail Killer: Jael

Many women do noble things, but you surpass
them all.

—Proverbs 31:29

I would like to continue with the story of Deborah and Barak and to understand the role that "the nail killer" played in bringing victory to Israel, but who was this "nail killer" and what was her relevance in this story?

The background to the story as told in Judges 4 is that Deborah and Barak had pursued the Canaanites and overthrew them, but Sisera, the captain of the army, escaped on foot to the tent of Heber and his wife Jael. Heber had affinity with Israel but also had an alliance of sorts with the captain of the Canaanite army. How do we know this?

Sisera knew where Heber and his wife lived; Jael welcomed Sisera into her home, but make no mistake, Jael knew that Sisera was the enemy of the Hebrews and she was cunningly plotting his demise.

Perhaps Heber had entertained Sisera and other Canaanites on previous occasions and perhaps Jael had served them. Maybe she had overheard the conversations between Sisera and her husband and Sisera had expressed how he wanted to destroy the Hebrews. Perhaps she was dismayed and disgusted by her husband's grovelling and cowardly attitude in not standing up for Israel.

Who knows what went on it that house, but what we do know is that Jael outwitted Sisera and she now had an opportunity to destroy the enemy of Israel.

Sisera felt extremely comfortable in her presence, so comfortable that he fell asleep. Then Jael realised this was the time to strike, to wipe out the enemy once and for all. She did this using what we would perhaps call gruesome tactics, by plunging a tent nail into Sisera's brain!

Yes, horrific I know, if Hollywood made the movie, it would probably be censored! However, the outcome of the story is that the enemy of Israel was destroyed and the people enjoyed peace for the ensuing forty years.

In Judges 5:24, Jael is hailed as blessed among women. A woman that fears the Lord, she shall be praised.

P31 Leadership Virtues

Jael used extreme tactics to outwit the enemy. Deborah, on the other hand, was a no-nonsense leader, her objective was to get a job done!

Consider a time when you have given instructions which may not have been welcomed by all.

What feelings did this stir up in you?

What fears or sense of apprehension do you face when you are tasked to deal with a potentially conflict-ridden situation?

What coping strategies can you put in place to help you deal with any apprehension?

What virtues could you use to influence the positive outcome of a potentially tricky situation?

8

Virtue versus Vanity:
Queen Esther

She brings him good, not harm all the days of her life.

—Proverbs 31:12

Women, how would you feel if the man in your life wanted you to put on your best finery so that he could show you off to his friends? For some, it may not be a problem; for others, it may cause some resistance. Let's consider the scenario: your husband asks you to do something, you refuse, he feels humiliated, you feel justified, the cycle continues until sadly, the marriage ends in divorce.

This was the case for one queen who refused to submit to her husband. We read in the book of Esther Chapter 1, that the King of Persia had "summoned" Queen Vashti to be adorned in her best dress, her makeup, to be manicured and pedicured—you name it. She was then to join him so that his friends could "view her"; some may argue that this was like being at an auction market. She refused to cooperate and the king was pressured by his advisers to find a new wife!

"Oh, King, if this incident reaches the newspapers, can you imagine the headlines:

'Queen Snubs King!'

'King conquers land and sea, but has no rule over his own household!'

No, sire, this will not look good for you, you must be rid of her," his advisers would warn.

"Yes, you are right," retorted the king, "no woman should be allowed to treat me that way, I'm the king!"

After a few lonely nights in his four-poster bed, he started to miss Queen Vashti and thought, perhaps, he may have acted hastily. His advisers soon recognised this and suggested that there were plenty more beautiful women in the province. They offered to scout the land and help to look for a woman that would give the king the due respect that he deserved. So the search for a new queen began.

Now the king had several women he could choose from in his harem, but his appetite to conquer extended further than the usual suspects, he was hungry for success and dominance once again and just perhaps, wanted to see if he still had 'pulling power.' Well, he was the king, what woman wouldn't want the esteemed privilege of becoming queen? So the queues started forming like the X Factor auditions and women of all shapes, sizes, nationalities, colour, and creed lined up for a chance to fulfil this once-in-a-lifetime dream.

However, there was one young woman who didn't show much interest in all this showmanship. Her name was Esther, a young Jewish girl who was one of the exiles (or a refugee) in the land at the time. It wasn't until her uncle Mordecai insisted that she put herself forward for the role, that she reluctantly stood in the queue with all the other hopefuls.

Esther's beauty was recognised, the king was very impressed with her, and she was subsequently selected as a possible candidate for queen. She took her place with the other maidservants and was enrolled onto a twelve-month beauty and fitness programme.

No doubt cocoa butter, coconut milk, fresh oils, massages, facials, manicures, deportment classes were all part of Esther's everyday regime. All this effort finally paid off because the king was deeply attracted to Esther and Queen Vashti became a distant memory.

So Esther was now the new queen and the stage was set for her to walk in her destiny.

At times, it takes the demotion of one person to facilitate the promotion of another. Unfair? No, not really, Vashti had gone as far as she was willing to go, in terms of what she was willing to sacrifice to enter a new phase of trust and obedience to her husband. I am not condoning her husband's summons to parade her in front of his friends, but she could have exercised wisdom and discretion in her response to her husband's wishes.

Esther, on the other hand, when *she* was faced with challenges, was able to see things from a different perspective and acted with grace, respect, and due diligence to honour the men that God had put in her life.

Now, let's finally explore how she rose to her call and consider that famous expression that her uncle Mordecai imprinted into her psyche that she was called by God for "such a time as this."

The Jewish people were condemned to die due to the cunning, devious, and manipulative behaviour of one of the king's chief advisers, Haman! He hated Mordecai and hated the Jewish people. He knew that he couldn't give the orders for them to be destroyed so he deviously influenced the king, inciting him to act and annihilate the Jewish people. The king decreed it and there was no turning back—or was there?

Mordecai would not relent on hearing the decree, so he went to see Esther secretly.

"Esther, we need your help. Haman, that rat, is plotting to destroy our people."

"But, uncle, what can I do?"

"You can go and see the king and stop him," responded Mordecai.

"But, uncle, the king hasn't seen me for nearly a year, and there is no way I can go to him unless he calls for me. I can't help you, uncle."

"Esther! What is wrong with you? Do you think that just because you are in the king's palace that you won't be killed? Remember, young lady, you too are Jewish. When the king's order is given, it doesn't matter who you are in the Royal household, you too will be destroyed."

Mordecai continued his plea.

"Esther, you have to do this, you have to save our people. Do you think that God made you queen merely to look pretty? Are you going to shirk your responsibility just because you don't believe the king will accept you? Don't you realise that you have come to this kingdom for such a time as this?"

Those words pierced Esther's heart like the shrill of an operatic top C and she realised that she had to do something.

Immediately, she called her maids and ordered a three-day fast, not eating nor drinking anything. She knew her time had come. She knew she had to meet with the king; she understood the consequences, but Esther had resolved in her mind that if it meant a death sentence, then so be it, but she must see the king.

Her heart was thumping as she approached the throne room, just one final pause and then she knocked on the door.

"Come in," a voice responded.

"Esther, how lovely to see you!" the king exclaimed excitedly.

"What can I do for you?"

All the fear and anxiety that Esther had felt dissipated and a fresh bout of grace overwhelmed her.

"Your Majesty," she said as she lowly bowed herself to the ground.

As he extended his golden sceptre toward her, he said, "Queen Esther, it's always a delight to see you. You are looking exceptionally beautiful today."

"My lord, I am your handmaiden," she gracefully responded.

The king continued, "Now what can I do for you? You don't even need to ask, I will give you half of my kingdom!"

"Oh, king, you are so gracious, but the one request I have is for you and Haman to dine with me today and tomorrow."

"Of course, we will, it would be our pleasure."

Esther left the presence of the king.

The banquet was prepared and Haman could not believe the luck of his gods. "Queen Esther has invited *me*, *me* to dine with the king. Surely, this proves no one is as powerful as me except for the king? But *that* Mordecai, why does he irritate me so much?" He snarled angrily. "I'll show him who is more powerful. He will swing from the gallows today!"

As the king and Haman banqueted with Queen Esther they passed the time with chitter-chatter. Then suddenly Esther's demeanour changed and she spoke with a tone and authority which the king had never heard before.

"My lord and my king, it has been decreed that my people shall be destroyed."

"What? No!" responded the king.

"I have come to reveal the real culprit who should be destroyed," Esther said as she pointed her finger toward her guest.

"It's Haman, he is the enemy of my people."

"What?" the king responded in shock.

"Yes, he has also prepared gallows for Mordecai, my uncle to hang from, but he should be the one hanging from them," Esther appealed angrily.

Haman turned pale—he was a dead man!

You can read the rest of the story in the book of Esther, but suffice to say, Haman did indeed hang from the gallows which he had prepared for Mordecai. Mordecai was promoted into Haman's position because he was not desirous to seek out his own welfare but the welfare of the king and the welfare of his people, the Jews. The Jews were not destroyed, but ended up fighting for their cause. This historical event is continually commemorated to this day with the Jewish Feast of Purim.

What of Esther? Esther fulfilled her call and purpose. We do not know whether Esther had children, nor do we know whether the king ever called her into his presence again. One thing we do know is that she accepted her responsibility to walk in her authority and fulfil her destiny and call for such a time as this.

P31 Leadership Virtues

Is there something that God has placed in your heart to do, but you have been running from? Maybe you don't see it in yourself, but others see something special in you and you decry the gift that is in you.

- Ask at least five people you know to tell you what they think your strengths are.

- What are the common themes?

- If these themes resonate with you (and even if they don't), ask God to unlock your strengths so that He can use them to fulfill His purpose.

9

What is in Your House? A Widow's Story

She is clothed with strength and dignity and can laugh at the days to come

—Proverbs 31:25

There is an incredible story in the Bible about a widow who had bailiffs knocking at her door because she couldn't pay her debts. These bailiffs threatened to take her sons as slaves if she didn't pay up (2 Kings 4).

Now if any of you have ever had bailiffs knocking at your door, you will know they will come up with lots of threats and sometimes false accusations just to get you to pay your debts. Obviously, this woman started to panic—she had no one to support her. Her deceased husband had led the family into massive debt and her sons were probably not at the age where they could fend for themselves. I suppose I would be panicking too! So she sought guidance from the Prophet Elisha about what she should do.

Elisha was a no-nonsense, matter-of-fact kind of guy, and as she told her story to him, he simply asked, "What is in your house?"

"Now what's that got to do with anything?" the widow must have thought. She responded, "I have absolutely nothing! Nothing, but a small jar of olive oil."

"Okay, go and borrow some large jars, jugs, and bowls from your neighbours, borrow as many as you possibly can," the prophet instructed.

Now I can see the confusion on the widow's face, can you?

"So, Prophet Elisha, you are telling me to go and borrow large jars from my neighbours? Okay, I will do it, I may not understand it, but I trust you!"

So she and her sons rallied round and collected as many bowls, jars, and jugs as possible and returned to their home, shut the door, and started to pour the oil from the small jar into each of the vessels until they were full.

How amazing? How could a small jar of oil, perhaps 50 ml or so, fill all those containers? The oil just kept coming! When she realised what was happening, she asked her sons to go and get some more vessels, but they responded that there were none left. When they had no more containers to fill, the oil stopped.

Elisha told her to sell the oil in the vessels, pay her debts, and live on the rest of the earnings from the sale.

There are four principles that I learn from this story especially in times of hardship and lack.

1. Don't panic.

The situation is not as bad as you think! There is always a solution.

2. Consider what you have in your house.

The solution usually lies in what you already possess. Your "house" could mean your domain or where you live, but more so it may refer to what you already have inside you. What gifts, talents, skills do you have that *you* are not tapping into? Draw on your intellectual, emotional, and personal capital.

3. Connect the oil with the vessel.

The vessels on their own had little value; when the vessels contained oil, they had great value. Theologically speaking, oil is usually a representation of the Holy Spirit. Spirit means "breath" or "life." The oil could not take on life-form until it was connected with a vessel. When God made Adam, he did not take on life-form until God breathed into him and he became a living soul.

What stops the "oil" connecting with the "vessel" in your life? Busyness, not listening, complacency? The list goes on.

In the widow's case, if she did not take the initiative and ask for help, then she would not have been able to accumulate the resources necessary to facilitate the marketing of her product.

4.   Don't pass your assignment on to others.

Your vision may not be someone else's vision. Elisha instructed the widow to go and collect the jars. The widow sent her sons. When she asked for more jars, they said there were no more, so the oil stopped. There are times when we are divinely prompted to do things, or start a new initiative or business, however, there are 101 excuses that come to present themselves:

I have no talent, no skills, no resources, no money, no worth, and no value! Someone else can do it better than I can.

Finding the vessels usually takes a step of faith. I believe that if the widow used her creativity, she would have found more vessels and the oil would still be flowing.

Believe it or not, you already have the 50 ml jar of oil, but what vessel are you being prompted to find right now?

P31 Leadership Virtues

What is in your "House" that you could use to develop your entrepreneurial skills?

What assignment are you called to fulfil, but you keep deferring or expect others to do it?

What further discoveries do you want to make about yourself, and how will you go about doing this?

Write a plan of action on how you will overcome any barriers and discuss your plan with your coach or confidant.

10

A Source of Joy: Abigail

Her husband is respected at the city gate, where he
takes his seat among the elders of the land.

—Proverbs 31:23

Do you put all your efforts into supporting your workplace,
working day and night to ensure its success? Senior
management, however, do not acknowledge your effort and
either decrease sales commission or increase targets!

This could probably cause workplace rebellion or strike
action in some unionised organisations. Unless a shrewd
negotiator like Abigail steps in.

I will tell you a little about Abigail in case you are
scratching your head, thinking, *Who on earth is Abigail?*

Abigail lived during the times of David before he
became king of Israel. She was married to a man called
Nabal. I love to study the meaning of names, and according
to Strong's Exhaustive Concordance, the name Abigail has

a twofold meaning. It means "father" and "source of joy." Nabal, on the other hand, means "fool" or "foolish."

1 Samuel 25 says that Abigail was a woman of good understanding. The original meaning of the word *good* ranges from practical, economic and materially good to the abstract aspect of good, for example desirable, pleasant, beauty.

Abigail also had the ability to exhibit intelligence, wisdom, discretion, and common sense in a crisis situation.

Are you still with me? Okay, let us focus a little on her husband.

Nabal, although he was very rich and had a booming business, was called a churlish[3] man. In other words, he was hard, mean, cruel, and deliberately stifling!

Now how could a woman of such beauty and wisdom marry such a severe, harsh, and stubborn man! What could her parents have been thinking when they put them together?

Anyway, come and explore with me for a little while and see why Abigail is one of my heroes.

Before David became king of Israel, he was very much a fugitive, always ducking and diving from King Saul, whose envious streak wanted to annihilate David.

David and his band of men were in need of supplies, and as Nabal was very rich, having over three thousand sheep and a thousand goats (probably a million-pound industry in today's terms!), David sent a request to Nabal as he heard that he was in the sheep-shearing season.

---

[3] 1 Samuel 15:7—*Authorised King James Version*

The message probably sounded something like this:

> "Hello, Nabal, my old friend, you may remember me. We protected your shepherds when they were in the wilderness. We never hurt them, nor took any of their belongings.
>
> I wonder if you could now spare a thought for us as we are in short supply of food and other essentials. Give us anything you can to help us during this rough time."

Hmm, how do you think a stingy, foolish businessman reacted to that!

Yes, you got it right! Nabal's response was:

> "Not likely! Who are you? Just a bunch of outlaws who have escaped from Saul. Do you think I'm going to take my provision and give it to you?"

When David heard this message, he saw red! Immediately, he told his men to put on swords as they were going to shed some blood, they were ready to take Nabal out!

The Shrewd Negotiator Intervenes

Abigail, not considering her own safety, immediately went to see David and his men. She apologised profusely for her husband's behaviour and drew on her unique strengths and abilities to appease David's anger:

She approached him in the spirit of humility.

Abigail held a very prominent position as wife of a wealthy businessman, but she saw fit to humble herself, bow herself to the ground and honour David.

She used effective communication techniques.

Communication is not just about words, but it is also about body language. It is said that 55 percent of meaning is conveyed by facial expressions and body language alone[4]. So while she stated the facts, her demeanour and presence complemented the words she spoke.

She took the blame for her husband's wrongdoing.

We live in an age blighted by a blame culture. Our workplaces thrive on pointing the finger at someone else, but Abigail said to David, "Please forgive the trespass of your maidservant." She realised that both she and her husband together were a team, so if he messed up,

---

[4] [Mehrabian, A (1981). Silent Messages. Implicit communication of emotions and attitudes. Belmont, CA: Wadsworth]

then it reflected on the whole team, and the whole team took responsibility!

She affirmed David and his call.

Imagine, David was ready to kill her husband and perhaps wipe out their whole business, but Abigail affirmed David and told him that he could not thwart the call of God on his life, just because of her husband's unwise actions. Don't let a fool stop you from reaching your destiny.

This action left David speechless! He blessed her and thanked her for her wise advice and acknowledged that her advice had kept him from shedding blood and causing hurt.

P31 Leadership Virtues

Do you work or live with a person who has similar characteristics to Nabal? How do you react to their behaviour?

How do you think you could work with your colleagues, friends, or family members to develop better interpersonal skills?

Have you ever thought of forgiving someone in your workplace for the wrong they have caused you?

Why not use the PEACE Model to help diffuse conflict?

Prepare

Before you address a problematic situation take time to reflect and prepare your approach.

Engage

Ensure you engage with the other party(ies) through questioning, listening, eye contact, posture, and adjusting body and facial behaviour. It is important to allow the other party to feel as comfortable as possible in order for you to gain the most out of the encounter, not only should you engage your head, but also engage your heart!

Attitude

It is said that your "attitude determines your altitude." If you want to manage and resolve conflict, developing a right attitude is key. What are some of the things that you can do to check and adjust your attitude?

Consensus

It is not always possible to achieve a win-win situation on the first or even the second attempt; however, what you can achieve is the reaching of a consensus with the other party. Consensus means agreeing on an outcome that you are both happy to take forward even if it is a compromise. The art of conflict resolution is achieving harmony despite differences and still being able to maintain a professional relationship with aggrieved parties.

Evaluate

Self-evaluation, reflection, and action are the main indicators of an attitude of self-improvement.

Once you have addressed the issue, then it is important to reflect on how you handled the situation.

11

Past Your Sell-By Date: Elizabeth

Her children arise and call her "blessed."

—Proverbs 31:28

Now you need to stay with me for this next piece. Are you ready? Good!

Do you sometimes feel that life is passing you by? Ladies, you may be wondering, when is it going to be your time? You may not yet be in that wholesome relationship that you dreamed of in your youth, or maybe you would-be mothers have not yet heard, "Yes, you are pregnant!"

Well, come with me as I explore the life of Elizabeth, the mother of John the Baptist (Luke 1). She was the cousin of Mary, the mother of Jesus, and the wife of Zechariah, a priest who served in the temple.

To cut a long story short, the Angel Gabriel appeared to Zechariah and told him that his wife Elizabeth (who was well past child-bearing age) would have a son and he should call his name John.

"Huh! Have a son? Are you sure?" Zechariah gulped in disbelief. "You may have forgotten, Angel, I am no spring chicken and my wife is well past child-bearing age and we are just getting ready for retirement!"

Before we go further, maybe Zechariah had a point. He and Elizabeth had probably been trying to have children for some time. Being childless in those days was frowned upon. To put it bluntly, it was a disgrace.

I suppose Zachariah and Elizabeth had just accepted their lot in life as being childless and had now resigned themselves to that fact.

But the Angel Gabriel came and upset the equilibrium!

What would Zechariah say to his friends and family—he would probably be scorned if he told them that an angel appeared and told him he was going to be a daddy! Well, fortunately (or unfortunately for Zechariah), he was struck dumb until after the birth of John the Baptist, so he no longer had a say in the matter!

Lo and behold, as the story goes, Elizabeth became pregnant and eventually had her son, who, according to Jesus, was one of the greatest men that ever lived up to that point in time.

I think there is more to this story than meets the eye! Why would God wait until this woman was well into her fifties even sixties before giving birth? It's not as if there existed the medical expertise that we have today with regard to surrogacy, test tubes, or fertility treatment! Well, here are the main themes that I draw from this story:

The Promise is Given

Elizabeth was the answer to someone's obedience. Phineas, her great-great-great (and the rest) grandfather, was obedient in carrying out the Lord's wishes according to Numbers 25. Because of this, God gave him two promises:

- a promise of peace and
- an eternal priesthood.

My conclusions are that all those years later, Elizabeth was being prepared to be a carrier of that promise in the person of John the Baptist.

Before I was born, my mother prayed for a baby girl as she had had one male child after another (eight altogether!). After she prayed, I was conceived. Yes, I am an answer to someone's prayer, I am sure you are too! Even if you feel as though you were not wanted, God wanted you here!

The Promise is Reinforced

The childless woman will have children. In Isaiah 54, childlessness seems to be celebrated as it suggests that the childless should start celebrating because they have more children than the married. Could this have been a direct prophecy about Elizabeth and John the Baptist? The clue lies in Isaiah 54:10

> Though the mountains be shaken and the hills be removed, yet my unfailing love for you will not be shaken **nor my covenant of peace be removed,** says the Lord, who has compassion on you.

The Promise is Fulfilled

Elizabeth's time had come. God's promise to her ancestors was fulfilled. It was time for the childless woman to rejoice. It could not have been more precisely timed as John the Baptist would be the one who set the scene, ready for Jesus, known to many as the Messiah.

Are you feeling like a failure? Do you feel as if you have passed your "sell-by date"?

One notable person that comes to mind is the poet John Keats who died at the age of twenty-five. He died a pauper and believed he had failed to accomplish his purpose, but his poetry has touched millions of lives since his death.

P31 Leadership Virtues

Maybe your dreams have not been fulfilled, goals have not come to pass, life seems physically, spiritually, and emotionally barren. However, we are encouraged to start celebrating even in times of unfruitfulness because with God, nothing is impossible.

One of the secrets to overcoming adversity is to look adversity in the eye and give praise even when you don't feel like doing this.

What actions can you put in place to remind yourself to give praise even in the face of obstacles?

12

The Mother of the Man Who Changed the World: Mary

Many women do noble things, but you surpass
them all.

—Proverbs 31:29

Very little is known about Mary, the mother of Jesus. Catholic tradition tells us that Joachim was the father of Mary, but no reference of this is mentioned in the New Testament. In fact, when Mary became pregnant, she ran off to the hills to stay with her cousin Elizabeth, no doubt to find clarity and meaning to all that had happened to her. Perhaps her parents disowned her, or perhaps it was to avoid nosey neighbours and even to give Joseph some space to take everything in! We can't be sure, but what we *do know* is that a teenage girl was chosen to give birth to Jesus the Saviour of the World.

Why Mary? Why not some other girl? Did God randomly choose this woman?

Well, scripture tells us that the Messiah would come from the lineage of David, his mother would be a virgin, she had to be engaged to a particular man also of the lineage of David, related to a particular cousin—I suppose that narrows things down a little, but I am sure there were quite a few women who fit that category.

Imagine having an angel appear to you and say, "Hail, you are highly favoured, the Lord is with you, blessed are you among women," but this still doesn't answer the question: why Mary?

This woman also had to be willing to say yes to the Lord and have a relationship with the Lord. So after much research, one answer that stayed with me was perhaps it was not just based on God choosing Mary, but Mary choosing God!

Let me explain! Mary must have already had a relationship with the Lord to be able to respond so willingly to the angel. Her song of praise recorded in Luke 1:46–55 is the deep expression of a woman who is totally sold out to God. I quote:

> "My soul does magnify the Lord
> My spirit has rejoiced in God my Saviour
> He has regarded the lowest estate of his handmaiden
> From now on all generations shall call me blessed

He that is mighty has done to me great things and
holy is his name

His mercy is on them that fear him from generation
to generation

He has showed strength with his arm, he has
scattered the proud in the imagination of their hearts

He has put down the mighty from their seats and
exalted them of low degree

He has filled the hungry with good things and the
rich he hath sent empty away

He has helped his servant Israel, in remembrance
of his mercy

As he spoke to our fathers, to Abraham and to his
seed for ever."

Now does that sound like the writings of a naïve peasant
girl? The passion and theological expertise that resounds in
Mary's words, expresses that of a seasoned rabbi. It sounds
like a quote from one of the great prophets such as Isaiah
or Jeremiah. The words resonate depth. The scholarly
expertise of being able to decipher between soul and spirit;
the prophetic eye of knowing that all generations shall call
her blessed; the passion and intimacy of knowing the might
and greatness of God; the wisdom of understanding what
happens to those who exalt themselves above God; along
with her knowledge of scripture and her forefathers.

This was no ordinary peasant girl, who lived in the sleepy
city of Nazareth—the young woman was far advanced
beyond her years and with the depth of her expressions,

seemed as if she had been preparing for this moment for many years. Even the unborn baby in the womb of her cousin, Elizabeth, leapt at the sound of her voice.

Mary loved and nurtured Jesus, until His time came to influence the world. She knew that He was only on loan to her and she had to let Him go in order for Him to fulfill His great destiny.

As Jesus hung on the cross, He said, "Woman, behold your son!" No doubt, many memories came flooding to her mind from the day the angel came to her to announce that she was God's choice. Memories of going to Bethlehem and being told there was no room for them in the inn, and, without murmuring, she would proceed to give birth to her firstborn child in a stable. The time when anxiety gripped her and Joseph in Jerusalem, thinking that they had lost their son in the thick crowds at the Passover celebration, only to find him influencing and debating with the great rabbis in the Temple.

Mary may have remembered times when, as a child, Jesus cried and she wiped his tears, when he said his first word and took his first step. But etched in her mind would be the gruesome picture of her son, hanging on the cross: had she let him down? If only she had protected him, maybe he wouldn't be in that position; if only she had convinced Joseph to arrange a marriage for Jesus, he could have settled down, had children! All the questions, all the memories upon which Mary may have reflected.

This amazing woman is aptly summarised in Proverbs 31:29–30:

> Many daughters have done virtuously, but thou excellest them all. Favour is deceitful and beauty vain, but a woman that fears the Lord, she shall be praised.

We salute Mary as a mother of mothers, a woman of destiny; we don't worship her, but we esteem her with honour inasmuch as she said "yes" to the Lord.

P31 Leadership Virtues

If you are a mother or a guardian of children what are you doing to ensure your children grow up to be the best that they can be?

How are you nurturing the children that you know or perhaps don't know personally, to enable them to be the fathers, mothers, husbands, wives, peacemakers, leaders, governors, CEOs of the future?

Make a commitment to invest your time, money, experience, and knowledge into the next generation.

13

Business - Where Secular Meets Sacred: The P31 Woman

She considers a field and buys it; out of her
earnings she plants a vineyard.

—Proverbs 31:16

We now return to the Proverbs 31 woman, and in this chapter, my key focus is on the entrepreneurial qualities of this woman, her business acumen, and its sacred implications.

What words or thoughts spring to mind when I mention the phrase: "being an entrepreneur or running a business"? Perhaps making money, working 24/7, or possibly even shady backhanded deals!

In our modern-day secular society, where materialism has cunningly taken its place on the world stage as the god of the age, it is difficult to perceive the possibility of business and enterprise having any spiritual connotation.

If we look closely, however, in biblical times, doing business was part of everyday life. Sowing, harvest times, selling, and marketing. Abraham, Isaac, and Jacob—the spiritual giants of the main religions—set the agenda in this area. As far as I am aware, there was no distinction between the sacred and the secular arena in Hebrew culture, it was all part of everyday life.

In my view, the Proverbs 31 woman was an entrepreneur of entrepreneurs, notably a class act in matters of enterprise.

The key word in the book of Proverbs is *wisdom*—i.e., the ability to live life skillfully.

The book of Proverbs delivers God's detailed instruction on how to successfully handle practical affairs of everyday life, in matters relating to God, to parents, to children, to neighbours, and in government and business.

This woman exercised integrity in all that she undertook, so much so that even her own children called her blessed and her husband believed her "price was far above rubies."

As women entrepreneurs, workplace leaders, or nurturers and home carers, is it possible to act with such integrity and passion in a secular society?

Absolutely!

Many ancient women leaders have demonstrated values, beliefs, and virtues that are no less congruent with the women of today.

A point worth noting for all women leaders within industry: remember, the P31 woman was strategic and global in her focus. As verse 14 highlights, "She is like the merchant ships bringing her food from afar."

She was committed to her workforce by providing a work-life balance for them. She valued and cared about her customers.

She made astute investments as highlighted in verse 16: "She considers a field and buys it; out of her earnings she plants a vineyard. Her arms are strong for her task and she sees that her trading is profitable."

This woman also understood and practised corporate social responsibility as "she opens her arms to the poor and extends her hands to the needy." (verse 20)

She remunerated and rewarded her staff (and herself) excessively as they were "clothed in scarlet" and she was "clothed in fine linen and purple" (verse 21–22). These materials were by no means bargain basement leftovers, but on the contrary, signified dignity and authority. I don't believe that her identity was tied up in the extent of her possessions but more so as a result of her generosity toward others.

Her time was not spent in idle gossip and chatter, but she possessed exceptional communication skills using words seasoned with wisdom and strength.

She was an inspirational leader, a great mother to her children, and her husband had full confidence in her.

P31 Leadership Virtues

You are a woman of noble character and God has invested something of Himself in you that will bring him glory.

- Consider the attitudes and characteristics of all the women in this book, what made then stand out?

- How different or similar were their circumstances to what you may experience today?

- What can you personally learn and adopt from these women?

If this book has blessed *you*, find three women that you can bless with a copy of this book.

14

The Designer's Daughter: You

Charm is deceptive, and beauty is fleeting; but a
woman who fears the LORD is to be praised.

—Proverbs 31:30

We come to our last chapter of this series and how better to
end than to reflect on you: the Designer's daughter.

I don't know the road you have travelled, nor am I able to
relate to some of your life experiences, but one thing I can
say about you is that I know you are the Designer's daughter.

Let's take an allegory of this concept—say, a woman who
designs clothes. When she first gets an idea, they explore
how she can turn her thoughts into reality. The material
she acquires is of the highest quality, yet its beauty is hidden
in its shapeless form. Nevertheless, with great skill and
dexterity, she cuts her fabric to create its own uniqueness.

The Almighty God is the greatest designer of all. Just
look at the earth and the heavens and you'll see why. You
and I are His daughters; we are one of a kind, unique in

every way, individually designed for a specific assignment, equipped with every talent, gift, and ability to complete that assignment.

The size of your mission has no bearing on how much God loves you. He loves you just as you are. But if you can stir up those latent gifts and are willing to be shaped by His hands, He will take you further than you ever dreamed. You are the Designer's classic, fearfully and wonderfully made.

I have no other way to end this book than to conclude with the words of a song I wrote several years ago:

Lost your identity,
walking in someone else's shoes.
Chasing another's rainbow,
Dreaming someone else's dream.
But consider for a moment who you really are
Designed for a purpose
To soar above the stars.

You are the Designer's daughter
Created by his hand
Moulded into something new
Chosen from creation
To fit the Master's plan
To walk in the path prepared for you.

"Hope!" that's what they say
Sometimes it seems so hard to do.
Friends, they will come and go
And the world may change around you
But consider for a moment who you really are
Designed for a purpose
To soar above the stars.
Soar above the stars.

Thank you for investing your time and energy in reading this book. May you continue to discover more about what God has placed in you so that you live your best life for Him.

References and Acknowledgements

All biblical references are from the *New International Version* (except where indicated) and Strong's Exhaustive Concordance.

The author wishes to acknowledge that these writings are based on biblical stories with the author's fictional interpretation and are not theologically based.

Acknowledgements to the Proofreaders:

Sonya Anya, Mother, Psalmist, Wordsmith
Pastor Phillip Edwards, Hope Community Church, UK
Pastor Claudette Simpson, New Life Christian Centre, Edgware, UK

My cheerleaders:

Denise Fox
Jacqueline Page
Avis Alagoa
Denise Isaacs
Delores Fearon

Dr Martin Glynn
The team at Carib Direct Multimedia Ltd

Acknowledgement and thanks to family and friends who have supported me on this project.

Heavenly Father, thank you that you have placed us on this earth to be a representation of you. No matter how good or not so good we think we are, You have the power to use those who are available to You.

Contact details
alinton@p31consulting.com
websites: www.p31consulting.com (UK based)
and www.hipcafe.co.uk

CPSIA information can be obtained at www.ICGtesting.com
Printed in the USA
BVOW06s2258110816

458603BV00006B/8/P

9 781682 375822